Man's Unofficial Guide to the Use of His Garage

Man's Unofficial Guide to the Use of His Garage

Thomas J. Neviaser, MD

ISBN: 1-932205-91-8
Library of Congress Control Number: 2003115590

Cover Design by James Baird
Graphic Artist at:

Word Association Publishers
205 5th Avenue
Tarentum, PA 15084
www.wordassociation.com

Dedication

I dedicate this book to the one true love of my life, my wife, Lynn. Without her support, love, perseverance, encouragement, and tolerance, I would have never accomplished this task.

Preface

One day, approximately 5 years ago, as I was admiring how my garage had evolved to almost what I dreamed of, I had this unbelievable, weird urge to write a book about garages. I am a writer of sorts but not really an author. I have written many medical articles, all of which I sincerely doubt you ever read. They weren't that interesting anyway, you didn't miss much, and, believe me, you will not find them in a bookstore of your choice. So, several hours before going to bed each night for what seems to be a very long time, I wrote the following pages hoping to impart the knowledge I had picked up over the years mostly from all the mistakes I had made. Mixing that with some humorous stories and remarks, I think I have succeeded in publishing a neat little paper back that you will enjoy.

The first few copies of the book will go to the closest members of my family, and then I will distribute some to those of you who, once you heard I was writing a book, encouraged me to do so and finalize it. The rest of the books, I hope, will sell.

If you truly like this book, tell someone about it. I'm sure they will like it, too. Thank you, and have a great time in my garage!!

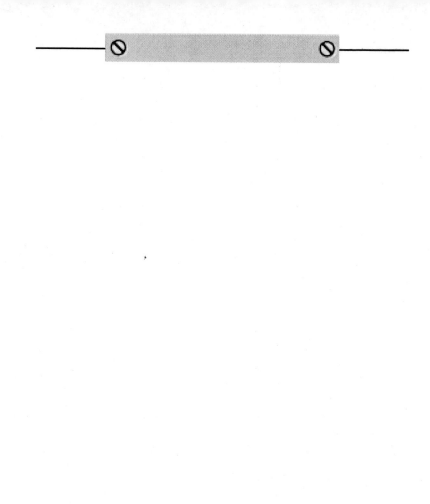

It has been said that "a man's home is his castle", but as everyone, especially a man's wife, knows it is really the garage that is his haven, his rest area on the highway of life, a place where anything goes so to speak, and his castle where he is king.

I have owned five homes, and it has taken well over thirty years to become comfortable with my garage. At this point, I know just about where everything is. No one else does, but I consider this the penultimate position to be in. Having reached this milestone means that no one else dares enter my domain for fear of destroying my overall clever construct of mechanical complicity and therefore reek the havoc that certainly will be thrust upon them, not to mention the possibility of actual physical harm if they upset the balance that I so fervently and painstakingly have established. In other words, someone could get hurt. Besides, if you set it up correctly, they will not find what they are looking for anyway unless the king allows them.

You may now be anxiously awaiting how many aspects of the garage there are. However, as all other guides before this, it seems obligatory to review and try to understand the history of the garage before we can undertake the "specifics" that await in future chapters. It is important to do this because I spent much time and effort researching the subject that you, my captive and totally interested reader, will have to endure. Of course, you could just as easily skip this introduction and ignore my discourse, regretting it for the rest of your life.

"Garage" is a French word meaning "a place where one docks". Of course this relates to boats. They appeared well before the car. Garage stems from the French word "garer" meaning "to make safe, protect,,or shelter". With the invention of the motor vehicle, the French started to use the word for "a place to keep a vehicle in". When the automobile became popular in the early 20th century, the British borrowed, actually stole, the term. Its definition in the Oxford English Dictionary is " a building, either private or public, intended for the storage and shelter of motor vehicles while not in use" and soon included " a commercial establishment that sells petrol, oil, and similar products and frequently also undertakes the repair and servicing of motor vehicles".

The first printed use of the word "garage" seems to have been in London from an issue of the "Daily Mail", January 11, 1902: "The new 'garage' founded by Mr. Harrington Moore, honorable secretary of the Automobile Club...the garage which is situated at the City end of Queen Victoria Street....has accommodation for 80 cars." A "Motor Garage" was advertised in the Times publication in March of 1902, and A.C. Harmsworth et al was mentioned in 'Motors' describing "the simplification of the motor engine and the establishment of garages...in stations or 'garages' where a number of cars are kept". As you can see, the garages originally were commercial undertakings for parking vehicles followed very closely by the repair and maintenance of these automobiles.

Later in the early 20th century, the human's love affair with the automobile eventually forced the owners to shelter their own vehicles from the elements, and man began to use his barns and other outbuildings on his property to protect his investment.

Hence, we have the eventual conversion of the tool shed or barn to the first "detached garage." Now, some of these detached garages were some distance from the house.

It soon became painfully obvious that whether it was a garage or street parking, most people wanted their cars conveniently near their homes. The increasing interest in the detached garage was evident in the Sears, Roebuck and Co. 1926 house catalog. While the company had over 80 prefabricated houses for sale, none had an attached garage, but six pages in the catalog were used to promote plans and the lumber for "detached garages" ranging anywhere from $86.50 to $274 for a two-car steel garage, the largest measuring 23'4" by 20'.

Sloshing out to the barn or tool shed in bad weather soon became a most difficult and unpleasant chore. Men probably were sneaking out to admire their prize and had to endure a ration of verbal abuse from their spouse about the mud and gunk they brought back into the house after their visit to their trophy. The poor man's answer was the carport, and those brave souls with a little more money added the "attached" garage. What an unbelievable and modern addition to their lives! Just imagine the first man entering his attached one car garage and under a dim light bulb seeing the second (sometimes the first) love of this life, right there, in full view, under shelter and gleaming in all its beauty. It must have been quite a magical moment. I wish I could have been that fortunate fellow.

There were no thoughts of placing anything else but this marvelous invention in this fabulous garage. On the other hand, there was no space to put much of anything else but one car in the one-car garage. I remember my father's two one-car, detached garages behind an old white-faced townhouse in downtown Washington, D.C. in the 1940's. It consisted of two by fours, a tin roof, and two rickety tin doors with locks. He had to squeeze into the garage, hard pressed between the car and the 2x4's carefully avoiding old rusty protruding nails, open the door of the car only part way of course, and slide slowly down into the driver's seat. Backing out was only an expert's job. He would check the wheels to be sure they were left straight when he parked the night before, check them again, and then he would slowly and deliberately accelerate in reverse while the rest of the family waited in heart-stopping anticipation outside the garage in the alley. The space between the car and the 2x4's could not have been more than 18 inches, and as the years advanced, and the cars became bigger, that garage became smaller, and the body clearance became much smaller especially if you were the size of yours truly. Of course, it was imperative to have more room on the driver's side so he could get in and out of the car. That's why we waited outside. The anticipation was really not for the exciting ride ahead but to see if he would ever run into the garage while backing out. My father's temper could rival a pit bull, and it was a scene to behold, but to my knowledge, he never did hit the sides of that garage. In the second week after obtaining my driver's license, I did widen that garage much to the chagrin and anger of my father. As I said, being an experienced driver just to get in and out of a garage was a must in those days.

The point here is that in those days, the car ruled, and garages were expected to keep these precious items safe, near, and yes, dear to our hearts. However, progress eventually overcame us, and men figured that there were other things they just had to have. Their companions did not totally see eye to eye about the exact whereabouts these items should be placed. Many moments of argumentative tension and face to face, lively spousal conversation must have taken place. The final resting places for a lot of those items were soon found next to the second love of his life in that tiny garage much to his chagrin. What once was a haven for his car was now becoming increasingly full of the other important things of his life. The answer was easy------a larger garage!!!! Too soon it became obvious that his important stuff was often times falling against and scratching and, lord forbid, denting his prized possession, his automobile. What to do, what to do?????? Hence, we witnessed the birth of the two car garage. A life saver !!! No, a marriage saver, don't you know!!!!! Now, the options were limitless, and we thank you, our sweet dear wives and companions.

WHAT IS A GARAGE REALLY FOR?

Webster's Dictionary defines the garage as a "housing for an automotive vehicle." It has already been stated that a man's garage is his castle. He is the king of this domain, right?? Do we men dare just put automobiles in a castle? NO WAY! If you want a nice neat space for your car and nothing else, you probably need not read any further, but you either bought this book or someone bought it for you, so you might as well keep reading. When you are through with the book, please be so kind as to leave it in full sight for the next good hearted soul to read, like on the back of the potty.

Cars just take up too much space in a garage leaving minimal room for those important things a man needs to continue being king in a domain so unfamiliar to the outside world. There is only one question here: What do you really want in your garage? Your beloved four-wheel chariot or those all important "man things?" The other question, of course, is: Can the car(s) exist with "man things?"

Since this book does not end here, you now know that the answer is "man things"' need to be in the garage, and the point of this book is to give some hints as to a cleverly designed organization of a garage so that you may have the best of both worlds. Now, this is getting exciting, isn't it! Follow me now into a world of garage adventure. This is going to be fun!!

For all of you who have enough of that green stuff to have a home with a three-car-garage, this will be a piece of cake, and you get to eat it too, but keep on reading, and you three-car guys may learn a little too. But, for you guys out there who are not so well off, you must use your ingenuity and basic survival instincts to obtain that ultimate goal, your dream castle, "the perfect garage." By the way, it will never be perfect. There is always room (excuse the pun) for improvement. That's what makes it fun. Move it there, buy this tool, throw this out, buy another tool, replace that, move it over there and back again. The fun is about to begin.

Chapter I

Floor Plan

If you have a one-car garage, you have a great dilemma. Car vs. stuff!! Which one will it be? I can tell right now it will be the car in the beginning.

After a short honeymoon period after marriage to that lovely young lady, there will always be a gradual increase of "man things" in the home, the enormity of which will aggravate even the meekest of women. Subtle suggestions about removal of such objects begin which, if not heeded, will turn to more boisterous rebuttals to your feeble reasons as to why you didn't follow those suggestions in the first place. The "man things" will begin to slowly appear in the garage whether you decided to place them there or not, and for the safety of your second love, the car eventually will be relegated to the outside to suffer the consequences of acid rain, sunshine, acorns dropping from the old oak tree, and the worst of all---bird excrement! That's what a car cover is for!!

All attached garages are just about the same shape. Three major walls, garage door or doors, and entrance to the house on the fourth wall, a window or two, and a ceiling with a roof coordinated with the house. You wouldn't think that a guy could make a big deal out of this rectangular appendage, would you? Oh, you misled, uninformed soul. It IS a big deal!! Can't you see the rest of the pages you have to read? So much can be done in the garage area that it is hard to think of where to start. I will start with the grand entrance to the King's Palace, the garage doors.

You have options with these doors: horizontal or vertical. The horizontal doors are essentially things of the past. You will see them now and then, but it is too much trouble to open and close them, lock them, and put up with the warping that eventually comes with age not to speak of the scrapping of the door on the pavement, the noise from which would send shivers up and down your spine. Then, you have to lock them, and classically lose the key or forget the combination to the lock. Does it sound as if I have already done all this? I am just passing on some advice here.

Vertical sliding doors are much better. If you are young and "strong like bull," you will not need the electric motor so nicely installed into the ceiling to effortlessly lift the door and put it down without a bang or physical injury. You will certainly not need the remote button just outside the house door to conveniently open and close the door, nor will you need the remote transmitters in your car to open the door for you when it's raining or you have a bundle of groceries to deliver to the kitchen. Of course, you will. No one is that crazy, are they? I guess some of you are, but there can't be that many. If you are like me, you will also want the sensors on these doors that reverse the motor to avoid crushing something when abnormal pressure is sensed such as a car, dog, or child. Not exactly in that order, you understand. Please be aware that your remote or remotes may well not be the only ones in the neighborhood. It is not a bad idea to change your code every once in a while. I once discovered that a mischievous son of a neighbor was opening and closing garage doors up and down our street at night as a prank. A garage door that is open without your knowledge all night is sometimes an irresistible invitation to strangers to abscond with an early Christmas gift. It is also a good idea to place the doors on your security system if you have one or if you are thinking or purchasing one. In that way, you always know if they are open when you go to bed, and if they open at night a sound should notify you of such an action. As for that little imp of a neighbor, I placed a call to his parents at 3am when my alarm system beeped. That ended that kid's fun quickly.

With a two-car garage, you have an option of one big, wide door or two smaller doors. I prefer the two-door arrangement. If a big, wide door breaks, it usually is in the down position for some reason. At least, it was for me. Now, you have the laborious job of applying all your strength to lift that monster and lock the mechanism so it doesn't come crashing to the floor like an out-of-control roller coaster. By the way, never fiddle with those two big springs at the top of the door unless you really know what you are doing. They are wound very tightly, and once let loose without the proper locking mechanisms, can impart such a force as to seriously injure someone.

On the other hand, the two smaller doors will never break at the same time. Just think of it. The motors are not connected by an invisible umbilical cord. The light bulbs within the motor housings don't even blow out at the same time. When I was in medical school, I was always cautioned never to use the word "never," but humans are creatures of habit, and we will always use one door more than the other, and, therefore, they will never break at the same time. NEVER!! The smaller doors are lighter and easier to lift and tend to do less damage to your foot if dropped. Be sure that the door has a twist handle to lock the door. This is not necessary to use when the doors are functioning, but it is necessary to lock the door in the down position when they are broken, and you have to wait those interminable two to three days or weeks before the door repair man arrives. Otherwise, you have given an irresistible invitation to strangers to abscond with another early Christmas gift.

There is a space saving effect with the double doors. The wall area between the doors is a great spot for tools. You can hang small pressure washers or garden tools here for outside use. The floor directly below can be used for especially heavy objects such as buckets for ice melting granules, cement bags, heavy bags of fertilizer, or a larger pressure washer. These items can be heavy, and you sure want them near the opening of the garage rather then causing a hernia carrying them around cars and other objects to get them to the outside. The ceiling between the doorframes and sliding door runners is a free space to hang all sorts of tools and items. Just be sure they hang well above eye level. You have heard of the phrase, "Blinding Headache," haven't you? While discussing the ceiling, let us not forget that the ceiling space can be used, but use it very judiciously for fear of falling objects forcing that dreaded trip to the emergency room. There are many safe, helpful, hanging devices on the market that will store all sorts of items safely and securely on the ceiling. A drop down ladder to an attic space above the ceiling is a good idea for the storage of things you rarely, if ever, use such as Christmas decorations or the clothes you have grown out of and think that one day you will wear again. Do not store flammable material here. Always install an attic fan with a thermostat to reduce heat in this area. Don't forget lighting here as well. It is a good idea to lay 4' x 8' plywood panels on the trussels so you can walk around the attic without twisting your ankle or falling through the ceiling.

Windows in the garage are a very important part of coordinating the outside of the garage with the main portion of the house in order to create a continued design effect and enhance the size and beauty of the house. I guess if there were no windows in the garage, it would look like a silly extension of brick or siding added to the house for the sole purpose of storing a car and might detract from the overall beauty of the home. However, how often and how long does one gaze out the windows of one's garage? I would guess not often and not long, if at all. Leave the aesthetic effect on the outside of the windows alone, but on the inside, I suggest a change. Every bit of vertical space in the garage should be available for use if you are going to use your garage for those "man things". Cover the windows with plywood and use a few but well placed screws to cover up the windows so you can remove them and the board at resale time. This boarding up maneuver also secures your garage from intruders who often gain entrance to homes through garage windows. And you thought you were safe with the garage doors down and the security system on. Also, it is always a bad move to keep the house door to the garage open believing you have secured your garage with the doors down. It is now safer to do so with the windows boarded up, and you have gained more space to hang your "man things."

Many garages are finished in drywall or plasterboard. If there is no covering, and you are staring at 2x4s, you are ahead of the game. Just cover every usable space you want with plywood. It is cheap and easy to work with. Use screws instead of nails. The reason is obvious. Nails are for coffins because they are so final. However, if your walls are covered with drywall, beware!! Drywall is what it says. DRY WALL!! Wall that is so dry that it will hold nothing. Oh sure, there are many fancy and innovative paraphernalia on the market to help you hang your stuff on that dry, easily crumbled, dry, drywall. If you are a master of all trades, you are just the guy that can do it. All the power to you, my man!! If you are not, and you are like me, we have failed more times than we are willing to admit. I have quit trying. Yes, I'm a quitter. I now automatically screw plywood into the studs behind the plasterboard and try to cover as much of the garage as humanly possible. A wall-to-wall plywood garage!! Sort of a neat idea, eh?? And super-functional, too!! What more could you ask for?

Well, now that you asked, how about 12 inch deep, locking cabinets that run from the ceiling to about chest high, an empty space below them, and below slightly wider, 18 inch deep, waist high, locking cabinets to the floor? Voila! You now have locked cabinets above and below you, and a small workstation or space on a counter that is placed on top of those 18 inch deep floor cabinets. These cabinets are best placed on the same wall as the house door. You can place those clear organizational storage boxes for screws, nuts, bolts, washers, cotter pins, etc. here, and arrange the upper cabinets for electrical items (such as bulbs, outlets, switches, etc), small tools, paints and liquids so when your marriage counterpart requests a "honeydo" as you exit the garage to go golfing, you know exactly where things are, the job can be done quickly because, when you think of it, the longest part of any home repair is finding the tools and objects needed for the job.

Then your wife is happy, and so are you because you are quickly on your way to the golf course to hit the little ball or the big ball depending on your ability, and no one is the worse for wear. Also, always keep the keys to the locked cabinets inside the house so not every Tom, Dick, and Harriett can walk off with them. There is nothing more frustrating than losing the key to the cabinet when locked. It is not so frustrating if the cabinet is unlocked, but, still, it is a hassle. Keep several pairs. Believe me, it is a great idea!! Also, know where you have placed the keys. I really have experience here.

No floor plan would be complete without talking about the floor. It is almost always cement, hopefully, sloping to the outdoors. Pour some water on the floor to see if indeed it is. It really should, but if it doesn't, and you are really serious about your garage, you may want to think about a drain. There are problems with drains as well. They need to be kept open. Once clogged, there is trouble ahead, but if you want plumbing to be an integral part of your garage, consult an expert. Don't do it yourself. You can always blame the other guy. Blaming yourself for being responsible for what you have done wrong is seemingly not a part of our culture anymore anyway.

Basic cement is porous, and that means it will absorb fluid. Water, of course, will evaporate and probably leave no unsightly stain, but paints, oils, stains, gasoline or kerosene, and other distillates will stain. Not only will the stains look bad, but they may decrease the value of your home to any prospective buyer who believes his garage is his castle, too. Besides, oil on cement does not absorb quickly, and gravity acts very fast when inertia is initiated by slipping on the oil spill. The answer is to paint the floor with garage paint, or clean up any spills as soon as possible. Believe me, it is easier to clean it up now than later. If the paint idea does not appeal to you, and you are concerned about oil dripping from a car on one side of the garage (remember, we don't put two cars in our two-car garage, do we now?), here's a neat, cheap way to protect the floor. Simply take a 3'x4' sheet of linoleum, attach a same size piece of cardboard to it with plastic ties, and place it under your car cardboard side up. Any oil drippings will be absorbed by the cardboard, and the linoleum will prevent it from staining the floor. Once the cardboard is saturated, throw it away and reattach another piece. Do not use linoleum alone without the cardboard. Just one wrong step onto this "greased lightning" material will quickly teach you the effects of gravity as well.

Last, but not least, we need to talk about the garage entrance door to the home. This definitely needs to be secure and fireproof if possible. The door should be solid, insulated, and preferably metal, with the hinges on the inside of the house so the door opens inward. Dead bolts are a must. A sturdy doorstopper mechanism to stop the door from damaging the inside wall is a must as you clumsily push through with a ladder to change that one light bulb that doesn't realize the length of time it should glow. Also, a nice touch is some type of message board on both sides of this door for both you and your spouse to remind one another of certain things that need to be done. I will guarantee you that if you do this, your list will always be longer than hers. That is okay because you gain many marriage points this way. Do not let the message board cover up that magnifying peephole you need in the door so you can check who may be uninvited out in the garage. I will talk about lighting in another chapter, but I will suggest that the light switch for the main lights in the garage be placed inside the home so you can flick them on to see if there is anything or anyone in the garage before you unlock the door.

24

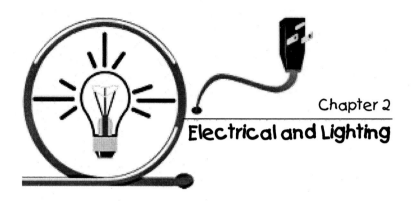

I am not an electrician. Actually, I am an orthopaedic surgeon. Yes, there is an "a" before the "e" in the spelling of "orthopaedic" because of the Greek derivation of the word meaning "straight child." Being a bone type surgeon may be close to being a carpenter, but certainly not an electrician. However, I do have great experience in never having an electrical outlet where it would have done the most good. That gives me the knowledge to impart to you in case you are or have been in the same boat without one or possibly both oars as I have been many times in the past.

You really should have more outlets than a contractor gives you if building a new home. If you are in an old home, get an electrician to add some more. You can't have enough outlets. Having the outlets 5-7 feet apart adds efficiency to your work and reduces the amount of extension cords you need. Also, knowing where the outlets are helps, too. This may sound funny to you, but cover up an outlet with anything be it a box or a board, and like magic, it is gone and forgotten forever. It is really a great idea to keep a drawing of where they are in your garage after you have inserted them in your new garage or retrofitted your old garage.

Now, check to see if you need GFI protected outlets. Your electrician should know. If you do it yourself and you are not sure, use them to protect yourself. Most outlets are located around the bottom of the walls, but it is a good idea to place some 4 feet off the floor for ease of access especially if you have shelving on the walls and in case water ever becomes a problem. All these raised outlets should be on a different circuit, too. They should be double duplex, 4 openings, and place one or two in the ceiling for electric doors and possibly one or two others for projects that will, believe me, come down the pike.

An electrician friend of mine once told me to be sure to let you guys know some important points. Outlets should be 110v, 20 amp. You may want to put in an occasional 220v circuit for a compressor. You probably will not need more than 30 amps in a residential garage. I have no 220 lines in my garage, and don't expect I will ever need one.

Do you remember that area between the cabinets on the wall adjoining the house mentioned earlier? Place 3 or 4 double duplex outlets here for the chargers of those cordless power tools that will be so important in your life. Why here, you ask? They are close to the house so you don't have to go far to recharge your cordless tools while working inside the house. That area between the 2 garage doors is where you may also want to place your electric pressure washer, the most wonderful tool to clean and wash your beloved car. It should have a double duplex GFI outlet here, too. See!! You can't have enough of them, right??

Now, I know there are guys out there that would like to have a refrigerator in the garage for that occasional "brewski", but alcohol and tools don't mix. I believe in the adage, "Never let friends drive a nail drunk." Now a freezer, okay!! I have a freezer for my upland birds and waterfowl as well as venison if I am at all fortunate enough to have a good hunting season. These little trophies probably never will see the inside of the house as long as my wife lives here, so I have a freezer in the garage. Lynn is an excellent cook, and she does oblige me and occasionally cooks my game for me, so I oblige her and keep the game outside. We also use this freezer for party ice and other frozen items that don't fit in the inside freezer. The outlet for this appliance is 4 feet off the floor and on a separate line, and this outlet is connected to our generator as is the inside refrigerator, inside freezer, well water pump, and a few outlets in the house for lighting when the electricity goes out for long periods. Isabel visited us in September of 2003 and knocked out our electricity for 2 days. We were lucky because there were some folks who did not get their blessed electrons back for 11 days. We never lost any frozen foods, our toilets flushed and filled, and the refrigerator kept the milk fresh for our grandson, Skylar. Take the hint, my friend, get a generator and have a well-qualified electrician set it up. You can get the manual pull start type, the electric start with a battery, or an automatic system that starts the generator when the electricity goes. You may only use it once, but it will be well worth it when the lights go out!! And, boy, did I get the praises from the family for thinking of the generator as our back-up. More marriage points for me!!!

It may be obvious, but I will say it anyway. NEVER place the generator in an enclosed space. Carbon monoxide is deadly!! You wouldn't start your car and keep it running in the kitchen would you?? The generator is always placed well away from the house in an area protected from the elements and well ventilated. Know how long the generator will run on a full tank so you don't run out of gas, but be very careful filling the tank with a hot motor. The time spent turning it off and letting it cool down will not harm the frozen foods and may well be safer for you.

If you prefer to take your chances without the generator, you are chancing your food spoiling, but even more than that you will have to suffer the putrid smell of spoiled meat that has defrosted to room temperature inside your freezer. The clean up of this mess is suffocating and horrendous especially if it oozes on to the floor of the garage. I'm sorry to be so descriptive, but I have had this scenic vista appear before me in the past. Experience comes from bad judgment. Hence, the generator and this book!!

Practically all jobs requiring electrical tools that are not cordless are almost always far away from the outlets, even if you have placed them as I have suggested. It is one of those mysteries of life. So, you must use extension cords. This macramé of serpent-like structures is not the easiest to use or store. There are several ways to win the war of these snakes: The recoiling type of cord retractor and/or a manual turning device that neatly stores the cord in a wire basket at its base, or the spring loaded retractor, good for 15 feet before it bogs down or retracts all 15 feet before you can plug something in to it. Actually, this does work quite well, but you do need to add another extension to cord to it to stop it from retracting as above. Always leave this second cord next to the spring loaded one and replace it there after each use. If you don't, believe me, the snake has won by the "divide and conquer" technique. The manual retractor has the ability to accept more cord, but it can be a drag hauling in a lengthy amount. I suggest placing one cord retractor near the front of the garage and another in the back. Don't be lazy and leave cords around on the floor or draped over tables and chairs. I think this is how the expression, "trip cord," got started.

If you are really into this garage thing now, you may want to add a telephone line, an intercom set-up, and get this, hi-fi wires and a coax cable for TV or video. I have done none of these except the intercom, but it would be so cool to have some, if not all, of these in my castle. I can feel the itch to run some wire right now!!

How about lighting for the garage? I know some of you have done the incredibly stupid maneuver of trying to get something done with low light or even a flashlight in your garage because the lighting was not that great, and you are too darn lazy to put in better lighting. Come on, admit it!! We have all tried. I can bet dollars to doughnuts that the job did not go well. Accurate lighting is essential and basic. Four 48 inch florescent bulbs in a housing are very efficient and light up well except in the dead cold of winter, but if you have enough of them and think about where to place them for the best effect, you can perform all the work you need. Have multiple sets of them in as many places as necessary. Don't skimp. You will need more than you think. Over certain work areas, you may need more intense lights like halogens, but florescent lights are effective if properly placed. Have these on a separate circuit, too. The reason is obvious. If your tools short circuit, you don't want to be in the dark at the same time. You could end up needing my professional expertise. One more area to run an electric line is the attic. That's right, remember the pull down ladder to the attic where you can store stuff you rarely use. You will need a light there to find what you rarely use. If you don't, you will never use what you rarely use.

As for all your small electrical needs such as light bulbs of different sizes and shapes, wire, extra outlets, exterior flood lights, interior flood lights, and extension cords, store them all in one of those cabinets on the wall near the house. Whenever you need anything having to do with electricity, you can find it there.

Heat in the garage is a nice idea if you really are going to spend time in the castle in the winter. Now, you have to be some type of hyper guy to do that, but there are some of you that will and must do it. Be sure to have a qualified electrician set up a system for you. You can really burn your bridges if you short-circuit this job. Sorry, I couldn't resist the double pun. There are safety heaters on the market, or you can have a set up of a 60-100 amp heating system to keep you comfy. I'm not that hyper to have any heat in the garage. I just use short intervals for work time in the cold giving me a break to go in for a cup of coffee. I know I will leave the heater on and something will go terribly wrong. No heat, no problems!! Besides, I use the cold as an excuse to not do some "honeydos" in the winter. Shhh, don't mention it to my wife.

While on the subject of heat, let's entertain the possibility of fire. A fire and smoke detector is an absolute must in your garage. Don't forget to check it regularly and test it. If you have a security/fire system, have the garage added to it. If not, please be careful and feel the garage door before opening it if there is any sense that there is a fire in the garage. If the door is hot, quickly exit the house in the direct opposite direction!! Don't forget fire extinguishers. Know where they are and how the use them. For small fires that may start while you are there working, have the fire extinguishers placed strategically around the garage. Remember that certain fire extinguishers are for certain fires: paper, grease, gasoline, etc. However, for fires in the garage that start without your presence, having different fire extinguishers near the garage but inside the house is a nice idea, but, if there is definitely a fire and smoke, first of all, get everyone out of the house and call the fire department!!! Don't try to be a hero!! I know this is most obvious, but my daughter, Julie, is a fire protection engineer, and if I did not give this advice, I would never hear the end of it. If she could, she would place a sprinkler system in the garage and entire house. Actually, that is not a bad idea except for the cost.

Chapter 3

The Work Bench

Ah, the work bench!! It is the king's desk that he can scratch, bang, mar, cut, hammer, nail, drill and smash with impunity. This is where you will spend a great deal of your time. It is probably best situated near the door to your home so you may get to it quickly. Mine is now directly to the left of the house door as I exit the home to the garage. The dimensions are really up to you. The smaller it is, the less efficient it is. The larger it is, the less efficient it is also because of the clutter that will eventually appear on it. My bench is approximately 7 feet long and 3 foot wide with a backboard of perforated board to hang all sorts of most used items such as drill bits of varying sizes, flat head and Phillips head screw drivers, a hammer, a few nails and screws, tacks, and, of course, several double duplex outlets with an 6 way extension, an extension cord neatly stowed away under the bench in a sliding drawer, a hot glue gun, a spot light, a small battery run screwdriver, and a battery charger for my cordless tools.

The top of the bench should be made of a one-piece solid material. I used to have a top made of 2x4's and all sorts of things fell between the spaces which were close to one another but wide enough to catch small nails and screws, just enough to frustrate me to no end sometimes. The bottom of the bench should have shelves as well to keep larger often used tools, but I can tell you right now this area will never be big enough. If you can, save your money to buy one of those red or black, multi-sized sliding drawer, lockable, organizing tool chests. Place this directly next to your bench. Now you have more tools ready to go whether or not they are large or small or used often or not. Besides, you will really feel like a professional pulling out that smoothly sliding drawer, replacing your tool, and then smoothly sliding the drawer closed. It almost becomes an addiction to do so. The key here is what has taken me years to figure out. ALWAYS REPLACE YOUR TOOLS IN THE SAME SPOT IF YOU EVER WANT TO FIND THEM AGAIN!! Oh, I can't tell you the times that I thought I had the brains to remember where I left a tool rather than placing it back in its place only to not remember where I left that tool. Oh, the time that I used up looking for that tool that I should have placed back in its place. Put those times together, and I would probably be 2-3 years younger not to mention the coronary spasms I have had desperately looking for that darn tool. Believe me on this one, partner!! ALWAYS REPLACE YOUR TOOLS IN THE SAME SPOT IF YOU EVER WANT TO FIND THEM AGAIN!! Okay, twice is enough, but in case you are quick to forget, ALWAYS REPLACE YOUR TOOLS IN THE SAME SPOT IF YOU EVER WANT TO FIND THEM AGAIN!! You got the idea, right??

The size of the tool chest, either the bottom with the larger drawers or the top with the thinner drawers, or both is yours to decide. Go check them out. Craftsman and Husky come to mind as makers of these chests. There are others that are cheaper and others more expensive Be aware that you can spend a whole load of money on these jobbies and bankrupt your piggy bank easily. I suggest you check them out, decide what you want, and walk out of the store without any hesitation, go home, and think about it for a week, then go back and buy. You will save money this way.

I am actually going through a process similar to the one above right now as I write this chapter, and I haven't bought anything yet even in the face of a fantastic sale that I would be a fool to miss. I am following my own advice. I must be maturing, but that sale really looks good, and that tool set I have been looking at won't be there tomorrow, will it?? Excuse me, I just have to go the hardware store, now!! No, I will heed my own advice. Okay, the feeling is going. The feeling has now left. My bank account is safe, at least for now. I certainly know how tempting it can be, my friend.

When it comes to security, you have a choice to make. If you can have a workbench with sturdy, locking doors and a solid thick board or metal backing in which you can store the larger and more expensive tools, you have quite a secure unit. If not, the more expensive tools can be locked in the cabinets I have mentioned in the last chapter. To be truthful, not all my large tools fit in the bench or tools chest. The wall cabinets are directly behind me and not far away, leaving me adequate access to them. The keys to these cabinets and the workbench are hidden wherever you think best. I definitely am not going to tell you and everyone reading this book where I hide my keys, but I have them in the garage and also extra keys in the house. I am also not going to tell you how and where to place your tools in these chests, but, for your information, your circular saw, Skil saw, and electric sanders do fit nicely in the bottom drawer. All your nail boxes can be arranged in the next drawer up. Oh, I'm sorry, I said I wouldn't tell you how and where to store things. Trial and error will eventually lead you to your own storage pattern. By the way, the glue gun fits nicely into the smaller drawers in the upper sections. Sorry!!

Working at your bench for a long period of time can be tiring. Place an adjustable chair with a nicely curved backing near the bench so you can just sit for a while especially if performing intricate work involving small maneuvers and small tools.

My chair has a work belt attached to the back of the backrest on the outside, and I sit on it backwards with my chest against the inside part of the backrest. The work belt hanging on the outside of the back rest is now a convenient organizer to hold pencils, knives, small screwdrivers, magnets, and magnifying glasses as well as other necessites to perform the job at hand. And, I am comfortably seated for the long haul. You can make the decision for wheels on the chair. It makes sense not to have wheels for stability sake, but, on the other hand, it is nice to scoot around the garage like a NASCAR driver for short trips to get other tools rather than getting up. I really am not maturing, am I?

Around the perimeter of the bench, I have placed hooks and one long magnetic piece of metal. While working at the bench, you may want to temporarily hang a tool within easy reach while performing another short task or, if it is metal, place it on the magnetic strip. Drill holes in one of the far corners of the top for the more commonly used drill bits and then mark the size of the drill bit next to the hole. In this way, you can measure a drill bit quickly without trying to pop your eyes out of their sockets searching for the size etched on the drill bit. You could invest in one of those metallic sheets with the holes already drilled and marked to measure drill bits, but again, if you don't replace it in the same place each time, you will lose it. The holes drilled into your bench top never get lost. Drill bits have always been an enemy of mine so I have devised a way to keep them in front of me at all times. I don't trust them. They are devious imps. They hide and lose themselves purposely to drive me nuts. Paranoid, you say?? Darn right!!! I have so many duplicated drill bits in drawers, cases, holes, and on the ends of drills because I ran out to buy one I thought I did not have only to find out later I had 3 of them right after I got home. So, I put them in plain sight.

I think it is a smart idea to have one of those small Wet Vacs on, under, or next to the workbench. It is a great way to clean up around the bench area, and it allows you to vacuum fluids as they spill. They are so handy to suck up loose nails, braids, tacks that often drop on the floor and tend to roll away from your discerning eye as you are just about to perform a very intricate maneuver. Mine is next to my bench on the same level as the top so I don't need to move it. Just turn it on and suck. The hose is a bit of a problem in small spaces and often jumps back at me as a snake, but if you slip the hose through the handle when you are through, it usually stays.

If you took my first grand idea I so generously offered in the beginning of the book, the one about plywood on the walls, you now have even more space to hang handy dandy tools near your bench for quick use. Take advantage of this space for those important tools you use the most at the bench and inside the house such as lightweight ladders, a 2 step ladder, long thin tools as a level, T-square, table clamps, etc. Do not place outside tools here. They sometimes are much heavier and more cumbersome than the inside tools, and you need to stretch across the bench to get to them. As you get older, you will understand the reasoning here. Until that time, just take my word for it. Outside stuff needs to be much closer to the outside doors, not over the workbench.

Lighting over the workbench is important. As I have already stated, 4 four-foot florescent bulbs directly over the bench with a stand by incandescent lamp or halogen lamp should do the trick. It is a nice idea to have lighting on different fuses. If all the lights go, you are up some kind of creek the type I am not allowed to print. If you have a little extra time, place a florescent bulb set under the top of the bench to light the floor. This area could be the darkest area in the whole garage, and to try to find something that fell behind or rolled under the workbench can do damage to your knees not to mention the headache when you bang your head under the bench getting up. I will guarantee you, whatever rolled under your bench, you will need immediately, or it will be the most necessary part needed for some project one day. Having this light will ease your tension better than extra strength Excedrin.

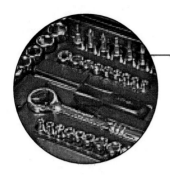

Chapter 4

Tools

Wow, there are so many tools out there that I have spent a great deal of time and thought on this chapter. I know it doesn't look as if I did, and you are just amazed at the fluidity of the words and the flow of impressive thought as you read, but I did spend time in hardware stores reviewing all the tools mentioned. I also know every one of you guys and girls have your own likes and dislikes, and many, if not all of you, will disagree with much of what I say. You really do not need to inform me of your thoughts, just accept my apologies that I left out your favorite tool. However, you know what? I am writing this book, and you aren't, so you will just have to grin and bear some of my statements and suggestions. I can please some of you all the time, but no tool pleases us all. Besides, you can skip the parts of this chapter you don't like, all of this chapter, throw the book away, or just place it on the back of the potty, but I'm still going to give my opinion about tools. Oh yes, there is one more thing you can do about your disagreement with me. No, not that!! You could write a book about tools and give everyone your thoughts, too!

I have divided tools into categories: outside and inside. From there, the tools are divided into MUST HAVES (MH), SHOULD HAVES (SH), the WANTA HAVES (WH), and the FORGET IT (no abbreviation here.) This seems to be the best way to approach the subject for which there is no end.

MUST HAVE INSIDE TOOLS

What tool would be the first tool you must have in your possession? I really wish this was an interactive book, and I got the pleasure of knowing your answers as to which tool you chose. For me, I pick the hammer: The claw hammer with a metal shaft and rubber handle. I do have another tool in mind that is really my favorite "must have" tool. I will mention it later just to keep you in suspense. While on the hammer subject, I think a rubber headed impact hammer is also a MH tool. How many times before I had one did I try to smash something into place and placed a nice rounded dent in the wood or metal I was pounding and still did not achieve the desired result because I was using a claw hammer. However, I did get smart over the years after obtaining my knowledge through experience that is always derived from bad judgment. I learned to place a 2x4 or something thick and soft over the object to hit with the hammer and thereby avoid the dents, but the impact hammer works much better. I don't wince anymore, and the dents are a thing of the past. There are many more types of hammers, and they would be listed under the category of "wanta have" (WH) tools in future chapters if I remember to do so. If you can't wait, go to the local hardware store, Home Depot, or Lowe's and check them all out. You will know right away which ones are MH or WH tools.

The screwdriver is next as a MH tool. Nowadays, there are combination screwdrivers offering all possibilities of shapes and sizes from slot to torx. Get one of these. No, get two of them. Separate them as far apart as possible in your castle so that wherever you are you are always near one of them. Since I come from the days where these little jewels were not invented, I still have various sets of individual slot, Phillips, square ended, torx screwdrivers all over the place. As you know they are hard to keep track of. The answer for me is that magnetic strip. Now some of my screwdrivers look like medieval weapons so the strip needs to be one of those super sized jobbies. If you have a wife or companion that tends to use other objects of extreme importance as a screwdriver, such as a one-of-a-kind, specially honed surgical chisel I had made for a specific surgical operation, you may want to place another set of screwdrivers in the house and let that sweet person know full well that those are hers and only hers.

A set of those small precision screwdrivers come in real handy when trying to fix small electronic devices or toys that seem to be made by really tiny people or miniature robots. Allen wrenches are a must nowadays but, of course, you need both metric and good old American sizes. Ever notice that you don't ever know which one to use!! Don't you think they should color code the nuts for us?? Anyway, don't get the Allen wrenches attached to a spring apparatus that is on a ring. This combo will drive you insane. You will inevitably pull off one of the wrenches and thereby stretch out the spring making it a monumental task to replace. Do this maneuver 2-3 times, and you will go nuts trying to replace it back on the stretched out spring.

Pliers and some variations are considered MH tools. Slip joint and groove joint pliers are all good standbys. They are better known as the "regular pliers with 2 settings" and the "long handled multi-setting pliers." I like these names because they tell me what they really are. When I ask someone to hand me the slip joint pliers, a glazed look of despair and wonderment becomes emblazoned on their face, but if I say "hand me the long handled multi-setting pliers," I have a far better chance of getting what I want.

Vise grips were the gold standard, but the new models available now are so much better, it is well worth looking into those than the old style. Pliers that have the ability to cut wire are twofold tools, and while I'm on the subject of metal, tin snips are MH tools.

Ratchet sets are next. Start off with the 1/4 and 3/8 inch sets as well as metric. The 1/2 inch sets are probably a "Should Have" (SH) or a "Wanta Have" (WH) tools, but I will not argue with you if you think they are MH tools. 1/2 inch ratchet sets are for the big nuts. No, not you or me, the ones found on large tractors and airplanes. They even come in larger sizes, believe it or not. Some are bigger than my grandson, Skylar. His dad, Bryan, is an airplane mechanic, and he has some of the most enormous tools I have ever seen. His tools have to fit in the rare category of FORGET IT for most of us. Buy your sets from a company that will replace them for life if they break. This is one great deal for us especially the way other manufacturers are slacking off on their quality nowadays.

The next all around tool is the utility knife otherwise known, as of 9/11/2001, as a box cutter. Every time I see one, I get a very sad ache deep in my gut and remember those folks whose lives were snuffed out by some lunatic with this tool. May all who fight terrorism be blessed!! Don't skimp on this tool. There are some very cheap ones out there, and they will eventually fall apart necessitating another trip to the store. Get a quality utility knife, and be sure it has a space for extra blades, has different types of cutting edges, and can be easily slid back and forth from the open to closed position without catching. Always cut with a straight pulling motion. Don't get fancy with quick or sharp curving motions. These blades don't like that maneuver, they can break and send a very speedy, airborne, metallic projectile towards your eye. Therefore, it is also wise to wear protective eyewear while using this tool.

Handsaws are nice to have, but with all the electric and cordless saws available now, the old manual handsaw may be an anachronism. If you remember these saws well, then you are as old as I am: the conventional saw tooth, the backsaw, and the coping saw.

I still like the hacksaw for those metal objects that need to be just a bit shorter. The jigsaw almost eliminates the coping saw for the normal guy, and the circular saw replaces the handsaw. The cordless saws are cool until the battery runs out 100 yards from the garage. Always have a backup battery charging, and I repeat the ongoing thread of thought throughout this book," Replace the old battery in the charging slot of the newly charged one." If you don't, you only have one battery. The Sawzall type of electric, reciprocating saw is absolutely a MH tool. It is a great time saver when you are building outside and need to cut thick boards that are heavy or cumbersome to carry. A long extension cord is a welcome sight and relieves the neck tension and headache associated with the alternative of lugging that board back to the garage and back out to the work area again.

The suspense is now over. I congratulate you getting this far. I know you read all the previous pages just to find out what my favorite tool is. The multifaceted, portable, handy dandy, cordless, 3/8 inch, heavy duty, variable speed drill is my favorite!!! A hammer it is not, but this jobby, more than any other tool I have, is the most versatile, light, and quick handling. With a quick release adapter, you can drill, screw, and even use sockets in its jaws. With the variable speed addition, you can use it for the heavy stuff and slowly use it for the gentle work. I just love this tool. It is the greatest weapon against the dreaded "honeydo." Wham, bang, you're welcome m'am, those honeydos are short lived!!

Obviously, drill bits are the absolute MH items if you have my favorite tool. But, which ones do you buy?? Black oxide, steel, cobalt, titanium??? Everyone of us has bought the black ones. They are cheap and so were we. If we use them sparingly, they are fine. However, when you find yourself drilling a lot as I did after falling in love with the variable speed drill, they got duller than a butter knife. So, get the bits that fit your habits. As you would expect reading this far, I have hundreds of bits because I didn't have a book like this to teach me what it took years to figure out. I learned shoulder surgery quicker than I learned this lesson. So there is a big box of dull black drills (I never got a drill bit sharpener) right next to my titanium set. I really like the brad or pilot point drills. They do not perform the jiggle dance off the center of the drill point. There is nothing more depressing than to see your drill bit spin off center across the mahogany board you expected to use for your wife's birthday bookcase. Not to speak of the searing heat across your forehead as you react and bang your head against the wall after seeing the gash it left in the board. Keep the bits in a case, and, of course, replace them after use. The metal snap cover type of case with a set of holders inside that flip back and forth with increasingly larger holes and size identification on each hole is nice to have. A variable speed jigsaw is also a MH tool especially with a quick-change blade system.

The next group of items are MH tools as well. A steel tape, at least 30 feet long if not longer, with a 9 foot standout. A "standout" is the ability of the metal tape to stand up against a wall without falling down into a heap on the floor. This has to be the coolest addition to tape measures. The first time I ever saw one of these, I bought two. Don't ask how many I have now. I will take the fifth as if that is an unusual cop out anymore. I will tell you I have more than 2 strategically placed throughout the garage and home.

The next item is a 4 1/2 inch workshop vise. No smaller than 4 inches!! Put it on your workbench in such a way that you can use it both from the left and right. Sounds ridiculous to say that, but if the bench is up against a wall on the left and you put the vise on the left, you will only be able to place items in it from the right and not very far into the vise before hitting the wall. If this is not clear, do it, but do not fix the vise in place permanently because you will eventually change it. Next, buy some clamps of different sizes: spring and bar type. You will always need them for drilling, gluing, screwing, cutting, planning, etc. Check out the types in the store and decide the best for you. The least number to buy is 2, possibly 4. Think about it. I like those cute adjustable bar types with the pads over the clamp ends to prevent creasing or denting the object. One side of the clamp can actually be turned around on some of them to act as a spreader tool. How cool is this??

Other MH Tools:

1. The wonder tool or a wonder bar: To pry boards or molding. This can be one versatile tool in the hands of an innovator.

2. A nail set: To set nails. Enough said!

3. Scissors. Get several good heavy-duty scissors, not one of those lightweight scissors that will bend in the middle with any force applied. ATTENTION: Once you have found some great scissors, hide them from the family. Use them out of sight of these people, or the scissors will disappear from under your very eyes never to be seen again unless you stealthfully search and find them in the house probably in the sewing materials.

4. T squares for right angles and straight edges

5. A level (a short one, medium size, and a long one). Yes, you will use them all!

6. A stud finder: unless you are an expert dry wall tap, tap, thunker. I always thought this was a cool way to find a stud but soon found out I missed the stud a lot. If you use this technique, find a very thin but stiff nail, and tap this into the drywall to check if the stud is behind. It this manner, you will not deface the wall too much if you are wrong.

7. A manual stapler: to staple fabric or other materials, stapling chicken type wire to a fence, and many other odd jobs especially honeydos. A staple half way in is a good way to

temporarily hold a fabric under tension after using a glue gun.

8. Files for metal and wood, and that one unbelievably named file, the bastard file, especially for sharpening knives, scissors, shovels, axes, and shears.

9. Carpenter pencils and the odd shaped sharpener that works so nicely on this type of pencil. Now, this little sharpener is easily lost. Besides replacing it every time I use it, the only way I can remember where it is, is to attach it by a string with Velcro. The string is pink so I see it right away when looking for it.

10. Knee pads: for those of us my age. The nice rounded fronts also let me rock myself up into a standing position so I don't have to stress the old knee bones too much.

11. Twine: You always need this. Get the pink color twine so it is easily visible. Hint: you can often use twine to measure if you have forgotten where your tape measurer is. I never lose mine, you know!!

12. 10 inch compound miter saw: If you have the money try to get the type that allows you to slide the saw back and forth. When choosing the place in the garage to locate this saw, remember that the saw will use up a great deal of space with this back and forth motion. They are definitely much more expensive. I don't have one yet. I guess I'm waiting for the price to go down. The price will never go down, but I think it may be worth the wait.

13. A 12 volt battery charger or one of those combined battery boosters or jump starters with a light and cigarette lighter-like receptacle. Get 2 of them, one in the car and 1 in the garage. I recall a 3am hunting trip marred by a dead battery. It threw me off my well planned schedule so much that I left my home in such a haste that my shotgun slept in that day. Needless to say, it was a good day for the geese. I also use it for a small fan for Ziggy, my Labrador Retriever, in his kennel during the summer months in the back of my capped pick-up truck.

14. A 6 inch grinder: I wouldn't be without this one. Great for the lawn mower blades and grinding down most anything metal. Use safety glasses here.

15. A flexible flashlight: Sometimes a lifesaver!! It can be wrapped around something so you can use 2 hands instead of one especially in the hard to get places, and there is no one around to help. It seems that everyone disappears at the time you need them the most. Am I the only guy that has noticed this phenomenon?

16. Gloves: An absolute necessity. I never bothered with them, but after many blisters, scrapes, scratches, punctures, rose bush pricks, ground dirt under my fingernails, blood tinged towels, sloppy mud caked hands, and a few choice words from my wife, I have learned to use them on almost every job. Yes, I still sometimes think the job will be clean and easy. It usually is easy but not so clean. Clear or colored see through "surgeons" gloves for those greasy jobs is also a must. Don't try to save

them when you are through. Now, that's plain crazy. I have been called that, too.

17. Cable ties: All sorts of sizes. Great little invention! Also great for temporary fixing all sorts of things until you can figure out how to really fix them. "Temporaries" often become permanent in my hands. To digress a bit, why do women have hair "permanents" and have to go back again and again for another. Isn't that a "temporary?" Just something I have always wondered about.

18. Electrical outlet tester: It speaks for itself. An electrical wire crimper/stripper/cutter, too. While you are at it, get the entire set including the spade, disconnect, bullet, and butt connectors.

19. Needle nose pliers: For some reason, I really don't use them much, but just when I think I will never use them, darn if that is the only tool I need to finish the job.

20. A Ladder: Of course!! A 6 foot light weight one, a multi-positional ladder, an extension ladder or one that incorporates all of these attributes. You will probably avoid a heavy ladder like the plague if you have one, so don't waste your money buying one.

I'm sure there are many more "must haves" that you are wondering why I am stopping here. First of all, it's my book. Second of all, the publisher has some say as to how long the book is, and thirdly, I am suggesting these tools for the average guy, not the Super Exotic Tool Time Guy. I know I have missed some of your most important tools, but some may even show up later in another category. I can't please all you guys all the time. Please forgive me.

"SHOULD HAVE" INSIDE TOOLS

We are now getting into the gray zone of tools. All this "must have" and "should have" stuff really depends on the jobs and the level of skill you possess. I really hope I have helped with the aforementioned tools as well as the tools coming up. Here goes!!!

1. A workmate table: This item folds into a smaller space than its size when open. I like that. It also works like a vise to hold larger objects. Some folks call them portable project centers. Hang it on the wall when you are through. You know, the wall that is all plywood!!

2. 10 inch table saw: To cut those larger than 6 inch boards or panels. Table extensions or portable rollers to stabilize the wood panel or a large object are great and actually a must. You'll find that out the first time you cut a 4x8 panel, and it bows right up and out of the cutting wheel. Talk about "What do I do now" situations!! It is always a good idea to have someone helping you if you can. All joking aside, use safety glasses here, never reach to the wheel to help cut the object, and if things don't look right, TURN THE SAW OFF. Don't chance seeing me in the emergency room. I have seen a few nasty injuries from this machine.

3. Bolt cutters: Nice to have when you need to cut wire that would destroy your scissors. Get double action ones for the power. Feel the power, man!!

4. A wall board saw: Nice addition to your tools for that hole in the wall from the door knob, my daughter Jody's knee, my son, Scott's fist. You get the idea. This saw cuts nicely through the dry, dry wall.

5. A chalk line: Neat idea but a bit messy. Especially nice to have to draw a long straight line, and your arms are too short.

6. A dremel: All those attachments, too!!! Maybe a MH tool!! Unobtrusive tool for fine work or getting into small, hard-to-reach areas. Great to enlarge the dead-bolt slot when the bolt in the door won't close correctly.

7. Hot Glue Gun: Great for quick fix-em-ups. The only draw back is the first and second-degree burns that quickly occur when the hot glue drips onto one or more appendages on your hands instead of on the project. A trick to avoid these minor burns, yet certainly major when they happen, is to have a cup of cold water available to place your finger(s) to cool the glue quickly and reduce the chances of a deep burn.
Yes, experience comes from dumb actions, too.

8. An electric sander: For the smaller jobs, a hand sander will do. There are triangular, electric sanders for smaller jobs as well. The larger sanders have several ways to put the sand paper on.

Some stick on, but this can be a problem while sanding. Others require you to twist a sheet of sand paper into one end and to tension the other end by slipping the small amount of sand paper left on the other end into a similar twisting mechanism. Now this is relatively easy with fine paper but becomes a pain with the coarser sand paper. A belt sander eliminates this, and you just slide the oval sand paper over the bottom of the sander and lock it. There is a little knob to adjust the belt paper so it centers itself, a feat that I have yet to conquer. Don't forget a dust bag for the belt sander, especially if working inside. My wife loves my working inside with the belt sander. In fact, when I really want my way, I just threaten her to use the sander somewhere in the house. This type of sanding begets some fine wood dust that drives women crazy.

WANTA HAVE INSIDE TOOLS

We all know what tools these are. These are the tools that we men stand in front of at the store and drool knowing full well they are probably too expensive, we will probably never use them, or we have no idea how and where we would ever use them, but they are so darn cool and would certainly look terrific in our castle. Now if you ever do get one, it will be too big to fit in the garage, and then you will have to disrupt your organization just for this one tool, and it really isn't worth it. But, it is a cool tool.

I saw my neighbor with one. This is another excuse we all have used. Believe me, keeping up with the Zalinskis, the Jacksons, or the Joneses is not a good tool policy.

Now, there is one tool that fits in this category, and it is something to drool, I mean, think about. An electric compressor!! My son-in-law talked me into thinking about one, and I thought and thought, and finally broke down and got one. I am glad I did. Now, it is easy to blow up the tractor tires, the car tires, and the truck tires, as well as remove lug nuts. These jobs were never in my repertoire until I got the compressor. It is small enough to fit in its own space in the garage, and the compressor's hose stores nicely on the manual windup on top of it.

A band saw is a serious WH tool. I have been toying with this idea for years. So far, my wallet has won the war. How about that lathe, drill press, and chop saw, too???

Oh, I could go on for hours!! Pardon me while I wipe the drool from my lips. Homer drools for pork rinds, I for tools in my garage.

MUST HAVE OUTSIDE TOOLS

First, let's get one thing straight. All these tools belong on the outside side of the garage. It seems stupid to say, but most of these tools are heavy or cumbersome to carry, and if they are way inside the garage, you need to haul them out and back, and that becomes a drag. Organize them so they are easy to get to and hang up on that plywood wall I have already discussed. Same goes for the inside tools. For instance, if the tool has a wood handle, drill a hole near your end of it, pass a rope through the hole, tie the ends, and now you can easily hang it anywhere on that ply wood wall. Those plastic cable ties I mentioned are great for this. For rakes and brooms, get two of those perforated (multiple square openings on all sides) square containers that are open on the top. Place one on top of the other, secure them with plastic ties, and now you can store your brooms or rakes upside down by placing the handle through the bottom of the top container. Organize those tools for use in the house and on the inside wall of the garage for workbench type jobs. Do it enough, and you will get the idea. Don't do it enough, and you will never know the difference anyway.

Here we go again. I wonder which outside tool you would pick as the most important. Well, the one I have picked isn't really a tool, but, without it, I couldn't perform some of the outside duties and clean up after myself: a 45 gallon durable, plastic trash can on wheels. Some trash collectors in our area give us one or two to use because it has a bar on the side, and the automatic lift on their trucks lifts the can and deposits the trash in the truck. I guess they deftly appear out of the night and repossess the cans if you drop their service. I think that is how they keep you as a customer. Somehow I ended up with three of them, but this family is certainly not at a loss for making trash. I am the trash-taker-out person and the dragger-of-the-trashcans-to-the-street person of the household. Wheels are great when hauling two of these to the street on cold, windy mornings.

The real #1 outside tool would be the shovel. There are a variety of these you really must have. I like the square, serrated blade for most of the digging followed by a serrated garden shovel, a floral shovel, and a drain spade. They all have their own specific feel and ease of use so I can't tell which one is the one you need. If you are into gardening and landscaping, get them all. After the shovel, me thinks you need a post hole digger unless you live on a very small property. On larger properties, you will eventually need a posthole, a mailbox hole, a lamp hole, or some kind of hole for something, and it will need to be 18 inches to 2-3 feet deep. Married to this tool is the formidable 70 inch tamper-headed, digging bar. This is one heavy tool, but it needs to be so because it is used to break up the inevitable brick, rock, or cinder block that is always situated exactly beneath the spot that I have chosen to start using my posthole digger. I am not kidding! It is absolutely incredible how I can pick the spots where the largest rocks live. I swear they move to that area as soon as they see me start to dig. There is nothing more bone jarring, jaw crunching, and arm disabling than striking a cinder block with a posthole digger with all your might. Digging bars reduce that vibrating, stinging feeling tremendously by breaking these materials into smaller pieces. You may want to work out a little before undertaking this type of job, but, on the other hand, this type of job may be the workout you need to get you into shape. Ibuprofen and a warm glass of milk will ease your aches at the end of the day.

Before I go on, please remember that your interests are not especially going to match mine. When it comes to outdoor work, there are 2 major types: "Honeydo" and "Iwanttodo." The first type usually involves smaller jobs but multiple in numbers often seemingly endless. These often appear quickly with no warning or thought. The good thing is that the tools needed here are smaller and fewer in number usually. Now, if these are the only jobs you wish to perform because you are not interested in the bigger ones, you just do not have enough time, or your philosophy of life is that weekends are for resting from the rigors and tensions of the week, then many of the tools to be discussed here are definitely in your NEVER HAVE category. However, if you are like me and you can find a task that absolutely needs to be done every time you walk into the garden or yard (hence the word "iwanttodo"), then listen up, my man, you possibly may learn a little. I hope so because if you haven't learned a bit by now, I have really failed in what I really set out to do.

Okay, enough said!! The next tool again is not really a tool but a super necessity: a wheelbarrow or something akin to it. Now, this item will take up too much room in the garage. If you keep it outside, think of getting one mostly of heavy duty plastic. Be sure to turn it upside down when you are finished with it so it doesn't become a swimming pool for little critters with the West Nile virus. A wheelbarrow with wheels! Note: I did not say "wheel." I used the plural. "Wheels" mean stability. "Wheel" means tilting, dumping, sliding, and ruining a good workday. Get a carrying capacity that is bigger than you think you need. Gosh, they look so large in the store, but get them home, and the fresh air shrinks them!! Get one deep enough to carry a lot of stuff, and get one with the insides steep enough to accommodate irregular objects. I like one-piece handles, not two separate handles. They seem easier to navigate through the yard and on slopes. Most of all, get one with sturdy tires. Most of the tires are filled with air, but if you ever have the chance to get one with solid wheels, get it. It is depressing, time wasting, and down right annoying to go out to do the job, and a wheel is flat. Less depressing now that I have a compressor!! Don't skimp on the price of a wheelbarrow. I have, and it was a disaster. Visualize yours truly, merrily pushing my wheelbarrow across the yard filled with dirt and shrubs when the wheel just falls off, and I am the farthest distance from the house. My wife edited this part, and this is what she said I should say rather than what was really said:" I am so very disappointed." Sure, that's the ticket. That's what I said!!

100 feet of outside grade electric cord, if not more, is a must. I don't recall 200 or 300 foot cords, but if they made them, I would buy them. The larger the yard, the longer the cord. Tandem extensions are frustrating, but there is no alternative sometimes. Actually, there is. Place GFI outlets strategically throughout your yard. I don't know anyone who has done that. I have a few, but they are not strategically placed, believe me. Getting back to tandem extension cords. There will always be that time when you come to the end of your rope, I mean, cord, and the two cords pull apart, usually while using an electric chain saw or something similar. Now you are 100 feet from the pullout. To stop these annoying happenings, twist the two cords around each other 2-3 times before plugging them in so the tension, when you get to the end of the cord, tightens the knot rather pulling the connection apart. There are also neat little jobbies in the hardware store to help perform the same task.

Now I know some of you have picked up on the fact that I mentioned an electric chain saw. Most real outdoor type men abhor these machines. They are cheaply made. They never last long. You need gobs of extension cords to operate them away from the house, and the cords always hang up on some root or stump. Granted, all these complaints can be valid if you are a lumberjack, but for the guy who has little yard work and some trees to contend with, it would be just the tool for him with less expense to operate and maintain. Gas driven chain saws are usually heavier, need a gasoline/oil mix in just the right percentage as to not gum up the carburetor, cost more, but are portable and durable. You decide.

Don't let the lumberjack inside you decide. I have had both. They both have their shortfalls. My gas driven one has been terrific. It starts with just a pull or two, is relatively light and cuts quickly. Here's the key: maintain your gas chain saw and it will take care of you. If you don't, be assured you will have rotator cuff problems, tennis elbow and hand cramps as a result of pulling that cord repetitively without success. You may become frustrated and go out to buy an electric one. Same theory goes for all your gas driven items. Maintain these guys!! You must read and abide by the instructions. I know you haven't fully done this before because men don't need instructions or directions, but this machine can do a great deal of harm. Know this tool inside and out. Don't expect to buy one of these (or a lawnmower, a weed wacker, etc.) and have it start every time without draining and changing the oil, filter, and the gas every winter. Don't forget sparkplugs as well. Keep it as clean as you can. If all of this is done, you have a chance of years of good function. If you are rolling your eyes at this point and saying "Yeh, yeh, get on with it," my retort is "Just do it and stop your bellyaching." My retort down the line a year or so will be "I told you so, I told you so!!"

As for the length of the arm on a chain saw, I think, overall, 14 inches is too small, and 18 inches may too big for the usual jobs to be done. A 16 inch chainsaw and as many safety devices you can get is adequate. Be sure you buy from a salesman who has actually used one and knows the problems first hand. Be sure the chain itself is not too loose or too tight. It has to have some play in it. Wear safety glasses, and use gloves. If you are going to be doing heavy-duty work, get some chainsaw chaps or safety pants just in case it attacks you. Do not try to use the saw for jobs it was not meant to do such as cutting out a tree stump. This is truly a dumber than dumb maneuver.

Okay, here are some more MH outside tools:

1. A pitchfork: For mulch, leaves and dead grass. Mulch and grass fibers run in every crisscrossing direction making it very difficult to use a shovel unless you are into getting into shape again. The shovel does not get very far into the pile and soon gets stuck against the grain so to speak. A spade pitchfork, on the other hand, will work much better especially if you have a long handle for leverage and for reaching into the back of a 8 foot bed of a pick-up.

2. A mattock: A 5 pound mattock. What the heck is a mattock?? Well, it has a slightly curved, heavy (5 pounds) metal end attached to a handle like an axe. One tip of the curved top looks like a pick axe, and on the other end, it has an sharp axe rotated 90 degrees. It will chop up hard dirt and small rocks so that you can then shovel them. They also come in two and one half pound sizes, but these are probably too light.

3. A rake: Get a good one!! Inspect the junction between the handle and the rake itself. This is the area that separates the "men from the boy" rakes. If it is flimsy, don't buy it. It will eventually bend upwards and become a useless tool. You may want to entertain buying a thatch rake that is more sturdy. One side of this rake has curved points for raking and the other side has flared points for cultivating, seeding, or working fertilizer into the ground.

4. Hedge trimmers: If you have hedges and bushes. There are 3 types: Manual, gas, or electric. You choose!! Those large, scissor-like trimmers (manual), if you have very little to do. Electric, if you have all the hedges and bushes next to the house. Gas, anywhere else.

5. Lawnmowers: I really do not have the time, effort, or inclination to go into these. Fact: If you have grass, you will have to mow it. Choose your weapon!! This tool may not fit in most garages, so you may think about a small shed.

6. Weed wackers or grass trimmers: For that manicured look!! Edgers are a luxury for all those neat freaks.

7. Loppers: These long handled tools are used to trim or prune trees and dead limbs. There are 2 major types: anvil and bypass (not a cardiac term). Anvil means that one side of the scissor type mechanism cuts down against a flat surface, thus the word "anvil", and the bypass is like a curved scissors where the blades actually bypass one another. I like the bypass type. The only disadvantage to this one is that, if you bought a flimsy one, you will inevitably try to cut a branch that is too big, and the scissors will twist and slip around the branch and get temporarily stuck truly eliminating the lopping effect. This would not happen with the anvil type, but the cutting edge on the anvil type needs to be sharp at all times. I like the 27 inch loppers as opposed to the shorter handles. Why do you think they decided on 27" rather than 24" or 32"? It's a wonder!!

8. A bow saw: For those short woodcutting jobs that you are just too lazy to get the chain saw. A 21 inch (it's a wonder where they got this figure, too!!) bow saw is just the tool. This saw cuts like nobody's business. A clean, slow, full cut is the key. You will really be surprised how easily this saw cuts.

9. Brooms: We need them. What kind?? I suggest a run-of-the-mill corn broom to get into those nooks and crannies where all the leaves and dust balls migrate and snuggle. Once the stuff is out in the open, use a push broom. The width is your decision. The weakest point is the connection of the handle to the broom itself. If you went cheap and bought plastic, the threads used to twist the handle onto the broom will eventually strip, leaving you with the handle continually turning in the broom that leads to chasing the broom with the handle, a neat little game but certainly a drag when you are seriously cleaning up. Two answers here!! Screw a drywall screw into the handle at the base so it also enters the broom casing, or spend more money in the first place and get a metal connector fitting that will not strip over the short run. Definitely find a push broom that has reinforcing brackets. The screw trick will save the anxiety and save money, but the reinforced model will last longer.

10. Trash Bags: I know these are not really tools, but what can we do without them. I used to be the king of cheap trash bags. I bought every one in the check-out line because I fell for the marketing ploy of "everything comes to he who waits in line".

Don't do it. Suppress the urge!! Get the bags for the outside and bags for the inside or use outside bags everywhere. These bags that are thicker than 1 ml are more sturdy. The paint or oil will not drip on the garage floor or spread over the driveway while dragging the bag to the trashcan. Get the ones with drawstrings. Keep the box of trash bags handy. Don't store them away so you have to search for them. Always keep tabs on how many are left, and, if necessary, buy an extra box. You do not want to be down to number zero when that all important time to have one presents itself, especially if it is wet, oily, or a slimy mess that needs that sturdy bag. Been there, done that!!

11. Bucket or buckets: Do you have the right bucket? I'm not talking about metal or plastic. I am talking shape. Get rectangular buckets if you can. It seems nothing ever fits into a round bucket very well except a cloth or sponge. Mops, paint rollers, small brooms, and tools to cleanse never fit nicely into a round shape. It is a good idea to keep outside buckets separate from inside ones because of the types of fluids that are used: oil/gasoline/kerosene for the outside buckets and soap, water, and clear chemicals for the inside buckets. Oil and water do not mix!!

12. Hydraulic lift: To raise the car to change tires. To lift up my 18 horse power garden tractor to change the deck, etc

13. A Pressure washer: Not just for car washing, but for the moss and mildew on the north side of the house, cleaning wood

decking, washing the drive way of ugly spots, and many other jobs. Spend the money and get the gas driven type. The electric ones are cheaper, and eventually they will leak their innards all over the garage floor that, if painted, will not bother you, right? Also, be sure you have long enough water hoses to get to every area you would like to get to with this marvelous tool. You use 80% less water, and you get the job done faster. Don't get fooled that just because there is pressure the machine can do it all. You will have to, for instance, wash your car to get the dirt off. Big globs of mud come off with the pressure, but the dirt film remains. Elbow grease is used here. Spruce up your deck every year with the washer, and if you are really a neat freak, remove everything from your garage and pressure wash it. Right!! I did it once in 30 years. I think I would rather move or build a new house before doing that again.

14. Hoses: Almost forgot these. I simply have not found the perfect hose yet. I just bought a" kink-free" hose. It kinked the second day I had it. The spiral ones are a neat idea, but they entangle themselves right in front of your eyes. If you want to store one of these, drive a 3 foot 3 inch PVC pipe into the ground and place the spiral hose over it for storage and less entanglements.

SHOULD HAVE OUTSIDE TOOLS

These tools are a difficult choice. There are so many we should have that they ultimately spill over into the MH bucket. For instance, the Wet/Dry Vac. The vacuum can be a small one as I mentioned or the deluxe large one. The small ones usually are for solid material cleanup and are usually not used for wet stuff. I think that if you are going to do a lot of different work in and outside your garage, the large one is the choice for you. My garage faces north so there are many leaves and dirt that get blown into my kingdom plus the fact I just may be a klutz at times especially with fluid type things. The deluxe wet/dry vacuum is really neat. It requires no filter and even pumps the fluid out of itself so you don't get a herniated disc lifting the water filled canister to empty it. I don't have one of these yet and so far I don't feel the urge to get one. Maybe tomorrow!!

Electrical outlets!! If you can afford it, get them strategically placed around the house and in the yard. There is no question that I have spent a lot of time over the years walking hither and yond to gather the right extension cord or two only to find that I need a third, and then I have to bring them back again when the task is concluded.

Unless you are truly electrically inclined, pay an electrician to do it. You will want outlets on all sides of the house, possibly 2 on each side and some in the yard and along the driveway. Why? Christmas lighting, car and truck cleanings, some of your electric tools, outdoor lighting, and many more reasons only you can come up with.

I spoke about a shed for the lawnmower, wheelbarrow, and other items too large for the garage. An easy to assemble shed could be the answer. Granted it is not really a tool, but it can be a tool shed. It will be away from the house so it would be a good idea to lock it for security and forget putting windows in it. They may look nice and cute, but they jeopardize security. Use the same plywood wall idea as I have discussed before to hang larger tools here as well. If you can, get an electric line out to it especially for a motion security light.

Other SH tools:

1. Sidewalk scraper: to loosen that nasty ice crust in the winter. If you have a lot of ice, get one of those small flame throwers that use a source of propane.

2. Hand truck or dolly: preferably a one-piece, sturdy, 600 pound capacity dolly with solidly based tires. Keep them inflated. Easy to do with a compressor.

3. Lightweight telescoping ladder: While on the subject of ladders, get someone to clean your gutters. I have seen too many orthopaedic injuries from just this one task except those that have occurred from falling off the roof. Don't think it can't happen to you.

Also, changing the light bulbs in the higher motion sensor lights around the perimeter of the house is a chore that you probably will not contract out. Hint: have an electrician place these around your house, each one placed above or below one of the windows. You can then change the lights from the window and avoid any ladder complications. Just don't work on your roof or gutters. That's what a checkbook is for!!

I really can't go on without relating a story of one of the first patients I ever treated in my practice with multiple fractures including a femur (thigh bone) and two broken wrists, a concussion, and lung injury. I will call him Clyde for purposes of obscuring his identity in case he is reading this book. Clyde decided to replace some of his shingles on the roof, and since there weren't that many, he felt he could easily do it himself. Having seen roofers use their ladders by affixing them to roof for their own stability, he decided that he would stabilize his ladder by throwing a rope over the other side of the roof and attaching it securely to his truck. He really wanted to move about his roof easily and felt this was an excellent way to slide the ladder across the roof and still maintain its stability. Actually, this is not a bad idea unless you forget to inform your wife that you have done this, and she drives off to the grocery store while you are on the ladder. Gravity always wins! It's not the fall, but the abrupt stop!!

WANTA HAVE OUTSIDE TOOLS

There are a lot of tools on this list:

1. A portable generator: to avoid the entanglement of extension cords.

2. Heavy duty brush mower: for the thick, pesky, prickly, high overgrowth.

3. An aerator for the lawn

4. A snow blower: After many years of drooling, my wife, Lynn, bought me one for my birthday. It hasn't snowed but once since!! Helped my backache though!!

5. Hydraulic lift trailer kit for the pick-up. No, I don't have this one.

6. An effective grass catcher for the garden tractor. Yes, I finally got this one, and it is very effective. It does not have an extra engine to suck up the grass. The grass is presented to its opening at the mowing deck's exit. Inside, it has a rotating wheel with 4 flat palms on a wheel inside its housing. This wheel is attached to my deck by a fan belt so it utilizes the power from the garden tractor. The grass is propelled up a shoot to the catcher. The catcher itself fits tightly on the back of the tractor. It has 2 tires for support that are able to rotate for ease of backing up.

FORGET IT OUTSIDE TOOLS

1. A backhoe: Right!!! My wife may just put her foot down on this one especially if I try to get it into the garage.

2. A Bobcat: Oh, sure!! I'll get this in the garage!!!

Chapter 5

Tools For Painting and Wall Papering

Plainly put: Let someone else paint and do the wallpaper! These two absolutely horrible chores have caused some of the most adverse reactions in my marriage from the sweetest and most understanding woman in the world. For some unknown reason, they seem to bring out the worst in me, and her tolerance with me becomes thinner than any paint thinner I know. Of the two, I would say wallpapering is the worst, but painting is certainly very close behind. There are some of you who are saints with unbelievable, laid back personalities who just love doing these hateful chores. I admire you all, and if I knew who you were before writing this chapter, I would have had you as a co-author.

As far as I know, the idea of painting is to get the paint on the object you are attempting to paint, not the floor, not on my clothes, not on my exposed body parts, and unbelievable as it may seem, not on my unexposed body parts. Wallpaper belongs on the wall, not on my wife's head or draped over my arm oozing paste on my wife's head. Wallpaper should be straight and perpendicular to the level although sometimes it looks as if it always should be angled. My wife never did go for that trick. For the life of me, I have never been able to get wallpaper straight and keep it up or paint without getting paint everywhere but where I expected it to be.

Therefore, there is no way I will give you any advice on this subject. I cherish your relationship with your wife or significant other too much!! That was an easy chapter to write!!

Chapter 6

My Queen's Perspective

I will now relinquish the writing of this book to the one and only love of my life. She felt that there should be a woman's point of view to this book. At first, being a man, I thought "How dare this woman!!", but I now think it is wonderful way to end this unofficial guide (as long as I am able to edit it). So please, give her a big hand!! My wife: Lynn!!

Hello! As everyone knows, women certainly differ from men in many ways. Women have the ability to adapt to their surroundings and are not driven by an adoring love of the inanimate, tools. (Hey, what about all those shoes you have!!) I apologize for the rude interruption of my sweetheart, Tom. My relationship with our garages has had a metamorphosis over the years. The first stage was utter hatred and disgust, the second was fear, and the third is an adoring love for his kingdom, the garage. (Now that's more like it!!)

If you are so unfortunate to have a garage when you are a newlywed, you will realize quickly how this extra appendage to your "queendom" (Nice touch here, dear!!) will turn to hatred. It is like having another woman vying for his attention and love. When I was far from home and needed someone to hold me and listen to my concerns, SHE was out there letting him do anything he wanted like hanging his beloved golf clubs on something he called "--- ---- drywall." When I asked ever so politely to have a picture hung, he left me holding the picture on the wall at "just the right spot" while he goes off to HER for the "appropriate tools": A hammer and nail, right??? Of course, while there, he must fall into HER clutches and straighten a few things up while I am still holding the picture. Pure dislike boiled to hatred of HER quickly. It caused me to do weird things like moving some of his tools so he couldn't find them and switching his flathead nails for finishing nails (So, that's who did it!!) However, luckily for all concerned, this stage doesn't last long. Children appear on the scene!!

Children now eliminate all hatred for the garage and create a new stage: abject fear. Years ago, friends from New York visited us. Unbeknownst to me or Tom, their son, Cade, and my son, Scott, played in the kingdom. The game they chose was to see how high the electric garage doors could lift them, a game that soon misaligned the chain to the door. We had the big, wide, single door for the 2 car garage that Tom has advised you not to use (Now, you know why!! Sorry!) The children figured there was just something wrong with the door itself, figured dad would fix it, and moved on to the sink in the garage. They climbed up onto the wall sink to look into the mirror promptly pulling the sink out from the wall leaving it hanging by one bolt. Later that night, Ed and Jan, Cade's mom and dad, were enjoying a tour of the garage after Tom realigned the garage door when Ed, who smoked at the time, dropped his cigarette ashes into Tom's tool kit setting it afire. The intense inner anger and exasperation seen in Tom's eyes at this point sent a fearful burning throughout my body. This is the abject fear I am talking about, the fear that others may become injured (Come on, now!! I wouldn't hurt a flea!!) when his kingdom is attacked, not the fear of the garage itself. Scott is now a veterinarian (Now he can care for our dogs free-of-charge) and Cade is a financial analyst with 2 kids. Ed no longer smokes, and we are still friends. No, Tom did not choke anybody that day (But it was close, eh?)

Unfortunately, more fear was to come when my daughter, Julie, began to drive. There really was no fear of her driving but an intense fear of an injury to the garage. Then, it happened. She hit the pedal on the right rather than the one on the left as she entered the garage for the first time. Thank God, Tom was out of town!! Tom's Billy-goat, used to vacuum leaves, and the back wall were dead on in her path as she plowed through them both. We disguised the wall and machine's crumpled remains as well as possible by hanging towels and tarps over them. We even swept up the drywall dust. Of course, Mr. "Know Where Everything Is" noticed it right away and that sense of fear once again erupted in me. Julie is still alive, being married soon, and is a fire protection engineer. Go figure!! (And really proud of her, too)

Our second daughter, Jody, is indirectly involved with Tom's garage. A friend of hers had borrowed her parent's Mercedes Benz (It had to be a Mercedes!!) and parked it outside the garage for an overnight stay. The next morning, Jody, having learned of the rage that could erupt from her father if anything happened in his domain slowly and deftly backed out of the garage being sure to be equidistant from the pillars between the double doors and promptly took the driver's side mirror off the Mercedes. As luck would have it, Tom was out of town. He always seems to be out of town when anything untoward happens. (Sorry!) She no longer was allowed to park in the garage after that, but she, too, is still alive, happily married to Bryan and with my "pride and joy," Skylar, my grandson (So much for being #1).

I must relate a story that has a happy ending for the garage. On a cold February night, a wonderful group, "Young Life", to which my kids belonged in their teenage years, met at our house for their monthly meeting. They removed everything in Tom's garage, poured sand all over the floor and set up a Hawaiian beach party with heat lamps, beach music, and bamboo. It was a wonderful party. When Tom returned (again from out of town), there was not a speck of sand or any inkling of a beach party in that garage for everything had been returned to its rightful place exactly as it had been found. Actually, Tom just found out about it editing this chapter (Son of a Gun!! So cool!)

Now we move to the third stage: total and complete love for his garage – his castle!! This stage began when he retired. He was finally home!! 30 years of being "on call", away giving lectures, working 12 hour days, getting up at 2am to go in for emergency surgery, and he now was available to me (How sweet, dear!!) Yes, he was there almost always to the point of being under foot. I couldn't get away from him from my morning coffee and the paper to the evening 11 o'clock news (Not so sweet, my dear!!) But then it dawned on me, the garage. Set him loose in the garage. So I have over the last few years, asked, begged, suggested, and actually pushed him into the garage (As if I need a reason to go there!!) Once there, he stays. He loves it. He thrives on it. It is a retirement lifesaver not to mention a marriage made in heaven for me and for Tom and his garage, his kingdom, and his domain. I love his garage, and I love you, too, Tom.

Thank you, Lynn!! I love you very much and appreciate all the support you have given me and for putting up with my trials and tribulations in the garage. I only hope all of you, who have had the perseverance to finish this book, have enjoyed reading it as much as I have writing it. Please remember to place this book in a conspicuous place when you are through with it. The back of the potty has already been mentioned, but I know that this book has inspired you to be innovative and creative. You could choose the coffee table, the guest's bedroom nightstand, on a bookstand next to a comfortable chair in your family room, or on your workbench. I'm sure you will find a great spot so others can enjoy it.

I also sincerely hope you have found some humor in it all and actually learned some interesting facts, tricks, and solutions from the unofficial guide to your garage!! Now, go out, and do the right thing!! Transform your garage into your castle!!